LOST LINES OF ENGLAND AND WALES
SHREWSBURY TO CHESTER

TOM FERRIS

GRAFFEG

CONTENTS

FOREWORD

Shrewsbury and Chester have much in common, with a documented history dating back to the time of the Romans, and have long been important commercial and strategic locations. Both are situated on major rivers, the Severn and the Dee respectively, and are on the border between England and Wales, a geographical happenstance which has shaped their history. About a third of the length of the railway line which links them runs through Wales. Whilst the earliest charter confirming Chester's status as a city dates back to 1176, Shrewsbury has always remained a town, albeit a large and prosperous one.

The Roman presence in Shropshire was centred on Viroconium, near the present-day village of Wroxeter, about five miles to the south-east of Shrewsbury, close to the River Severn, and on Watling Street, the Roman road which ran through London to the channel coast. Established initially as a fort around 55 AD, at its peak Viroconium was one of the largest Roman towns in Britannia. With the end of Roman governance in Britain, the first settlement of what became Shrewsbury dates from the time of the Anglo-Saxon kingdom of Mercia. Set in a loop of the River Severn within which was high ground commanding fords over the river, the strategic importance of Shrewsbury was also realised by the invading Normans and a castle was built there by Roger de Montgomery in the 1070s.

Chester's Roman origins were not dissimilar. Named by them Deva Victrix, a fortress was established there some time after 70 AD as the Romans pushed north to control more of Britain. In time it was expanded to become one of the largest Roman fortifications in the country garrisoned by the 20th Legion. A thriving port and a large civilian settlement soon followed. The Anglo-Saxons filled the vacuum left by the departing Romans and in turn the Normans built a castle and created the earldom of Chester.

With the coming of what historians would later describe as the Industrial Revolution, both

Shrewsbury and Chester were linked to the canal network, though neither place really was to develop as a major industrial centre. However, the coming of the railways revitalised them and in time both places became major junctions. The line linking them was the first railway to open in Shropshire and its fortunes waned with the cutbacks and closures of the 1960s and 70s which saw the northern part of the route being reduced to a single track, something thankfully partly reversed in recent years.

This pictorial journey along what remains an attractive and scenic line focuses on its heyday in the age of steam-hauled trains, when most of its numerous stations and halts were still open, goods yards were busy, the collieries it served were still producing coal and its trains were controlled from the many signal boxes alongside its tracks. Whilst the expresses from Paddington to the Mersey and the through trains to the south coast which it once carried are no more and much of the infrastructure of the steam age has been swept away, the line is still busy and remains a vital transport link along the northern border of England and Wales.

INTRODUCTION

The first railway to serve Chester was a product of that period of intense railway promotion and speculation in the 1830s often referred to the railway mania. The Chester & Crewe Railway was authorised in 1837. However, before it opened in 1840, it was acquired by the Grand Junction Railway which it met at Crewe. The GJR was the line linking Birmingham to the pioneering Liverpool & Manchester Railway north of Warrington. In turn, the GJR would make a connection at Birmingham with the London & Birmingham line, allowing through travel from the capital to the two major cities in the north west. Between them these lines provided the major vertebrae of the developing national network. The importance of the Crewe to Chester line was further reinforced when the Chester & Holyhead Railway was authorised in 1844, establishing this as the main route to Ireland both for passengers and the mails.

In Shropshire, thoughts were also turning to bringing railways to the county. The most obvious line was one from Shrewsbury to connect with the GJR at Wolverhampton, and to achieve this the Shrewsbury & Birmingham Railway was authorised by Parliament in 1846. Despite the S&B having a head start, the first railway to reach Shrewsbury was to be the connection to Chester though the origins of this were to be found further north.

There was an abundance of coal in north-east Wales stretching in an arc from the coast of Flintshire through Denbighshire to Wrexham and Ruabon. Ironworks also flourished in this area from the middle of the eighteenth century. The one thing holding back these industries was the lack of a good network of roads and canals to transport the coal and other products. To address this, the North Wales Mineral Railway was incorporated in 1844 to build a line from Wrexham through Rossett to a wharf on the River Dee outside Chester. The line would also join the C&H to reach the city. In 1845 further extensions were authorised, extending the line five miles south of

Wrexham to Ruabon and with other branches into the coalfields west of Wrexham.

Railway promotion in the 1840s and indeed throughout the nineteenth century was marked by frequent disagreements between the various companies as they sought to carve out territory for themselves and exclude competitors. Consequences of this could include frequent litigation, occasional direct action on the ground and the promotion of unnecessary lines mainly intended to thwart competitors. At this time the L&B was in conflict with the GJR and in 1845 promoted the Chester & Shropshire Junction to link Shrewsbury and Chester to bypass the GJR's route to the north. This was a threat to the nascent NWM, which reacted by promoting a separate company, the Shrewsbury, Oswestry & Chester Junction Railway, which was authorised in June 1845 to build a line from Ruabon to Shrewsbury. Later acts passed in July 1846 allowed the SO&C to build a branch from Leaton, north of Shrewsbury, to Wem, which was never pursued, a line from Gobowen to Oswestry which opened in December 1848, a joint station with the Shrewsbury & Birmingham and the Shrewsbury & Hereford companies in Shrewsbury and also amalgamated the NMR and the SO&C to form the Shrewsbury & Chester Railway.

The driving force behind the NWM, who became the engineer for the S&C, was Henry Robinson. Born in Banff in 1816, he was educated at Aberdeen University and began his career as a railway contractor in Scotland. He moved to north Wales in 1842, where he revived the moribund Brymbo Iron Works. It was his desire to improve communications in the area that led him to promote the NWM. As well as being engineer for the S&C, he also worked for the S&H and the S&B and was responsible for a number of other railways in north Wales including those from Ruabon to Dolgellau and Bala to Blaenau Festiniog. He was one of the founders of that famous Manchester firm of locomotive builders Beyer, Peacock and Company and also a politician who had two spells as the Liberal MP for Shrewsbury in the 1860s and 70s. The contractor appointed to construct the line was Thomas Brassey, one of the great railway builders of the Victorian era whose credits in Britain would include much of what is the present-day West Coast Main Line, the Chester & Holyhead Railway, as well as lines in many European countries and in Canada and South America.

Construction of the original NWM part of the line was relatively straightforward and services began in November 1846 between Ruabon and Chester with trains calling at Wrexham, Gresford, Rossett and Saltney. Access to Chester was via the eastern section of the as yet incomplete C&H line. There were, however, considerable engineering challenges south of Ruabon. Two great viaducts were required at Cefn to take the line over the River Dee and at Chirk to span the Ceiriog valley. The Cefn viaduct has 19 arches, is 1,508ft in length and stands 147ft above the level of the river. The viaduct at Chirk is 849ft long and has 16 arches; it is parallel with and higher than the earlier aqueduct designed by Thomas Telford, which was completed in 1801 to carry the Llangollen Canal over the valley. Difficulties were also encountered on the approach to Shrewsbury where the line had to pass through wet and marshy land to reach the town. Robertson managed to find stable footing for his railway using brushwood rafts supported on wooden piles.

By the middle of 1848 the line was complete to Coton Hill on the outskirts of Shrewsbury and services began from a temporary station just north of the present one in October of that year. The short branch off the main line, from Gobowen to Oswestry, was opened in December. South of Ruabon stations were provided at Cefn, Llangollen Road, Chirk, Preesgweene, Gobowen, Whittington, Rednal, Baschurch and Leaton. The opening of a new railway in the mid-nineteenth century was often accompanied by banquets for the directors, their friends and local bigwigs. To mark the arrival of Shrewsbury on the railway map of Britain, an opening special was run to take the great and the good from there to Chester, reportedly consisting of 39 carriages hauled by three locomotives. On its eventual return there was a banquet and a ball for the toffs and a fireworks display for the plebs.

The S&C's line was the first of the four railway companies approaching Shrewsbury to open to the public. The other three were the Shrewsbury & Hereford, Shrewsbury & Birmingham and the Shropshire Union Railways and Canal Company, which was building a line from Shrewsbury to Stafford. The four agreed to share the costs of building a joint station on a cramped site hemmed in by the River Severn and Shrewsbury Castle. This was designed by the Oswestry architect

Thomas Penson and built by Thomas Brassey. With the S&C open for traffic and other lines approaching Shrewsbury all under construction, the way ahead for the company looked positive. At the Chester end, C&H services as far as Bangor commenced in May 1848 and a joint station for all the lines converging on that city opened in August of the same year. However, the S&C was about to become embroiled in a vicious spate of railway politics which needs to be recounted, as its outcome was to have a major bearing on the fate of the railway in the years to come.

The opening of the S&C coincided with the collapse in the value of railway shares, which had boomed in the mid 1840s in a spree of frenzied speculation. This was followed by a period in which many of the smaller companies were swallowed up by or amalgamated with their larger rivals. The S&C had already been having discussions with the S&B as together the two companies were well placed to provide an alternative route from the Midlands to the Mersey to that offered by the London & North Western Railway. The LNWR, itself formed in an amalgamation in 1846 of the London &

Birmingham, the Manchester & Birmingham and the GJR, had a monopoly of traffic from London to the northwest, though this was being challenged by a Great Western line being promoted from Oxford to Birmingham. The two companies based in Shrewsbury were dependent on the LNWR and its allies for traffic to destinations beyond Chester and Wolverhampton and it was a dangerous opponent, probably the biggest railway company anywhere in the world at that time. The LNWR hoped to coerce the two companies into an amalgamation. It was building the Stour Valley line from Wolverhampton to Birmingham at this time which was to be the outlet to the rest of the country for S&B traffic but deliberately delayed the construction of this to disrupt the S&B. In desperation in 1850, the S&B built a siding to a wharf on the Birmingham Canal at Wolverhampton so that its goods traffic could complete its journey to that city by water. This led to a fracas when LNWR employees began to physically disrupt the unloading of the first S&B goods train at the wharf. The mayor of Wolverhampton had to call in the militia and read the Riot Act to restore the peace. At Chester the S&C also had to face deliberate disruption and obstruction of its traffic by the LNWR and its allies against which it had to resort to court injunctions.

Despite the ruinous financial consequences of the LNWR's activities, the two Shrewsbury companies fought on and eventually found salvation in the GWR, which was extending its broad-gauge line from Oxford to Birmingham and on to Wolverhampton. An agreement with the GWR was reached, as was a future amalgamation with that company. The heavy-handed tactics of the LNWR had completely backfired and the consequences of this were profound on several levels. The S&C and S&B amalgamated with the GWR in 1854 and the company which owned the line from Chester to Birkenhead also allowed through traffic off the S&C line to pass unhindered. An Act of 1861 conferred ownership of this line to the GWR and LNWR jointly. In time the route from Shrewsbury to Wolverhampton also became jointly owned by the two companies, but that from Shrewsbury to Saltney Junction, outside Chester, was always the sole property of the GWR.

There was now an alternative to the LNWR route for traffic from London and the rest of the country, via the S&C, to the banks of the Mersey. However,

another consequence of the GWR takeover of the Shrewsbury companies was that it was prevented by Parliament from extending its 7ft broad gauge beyond Wolverhampton. The locomotives and rolling stock acquired from the S&C and the S&B were the first non-broad-gauge vehicles owned by the GWR. By this stage even the legislature had woken up to the chaos being caused by sections the national railway network being operated on different gauges. A third rail was added to the tracks from Wolverhampton through to Paddington by October 1861, which allowed the first through standard-gauge, or in GWR terms narrow-gauge, trains between London and Birkenhead to operate. In some ways this episode can be seen as the high-water mark of Brunel's broad gauge, which was in decline henceforth and eventually finally abolished in 1892.

The GWR steadily developed the line throughout the rest of the nineteenth century. Three main traffic flows can be identified. Firstly, there were the through trains from Paddington to Birkenhead. These were speeded up considerably in 1880 when a new fast express was introduced, nicknamed the *Zulu*, which did the journey in just over five hours. In March 1892 the first ever GWR gangwayed corridor carriages, steam heated and with separate lavatories for ladies and gentlemen, entered service on the Paddington to Shrewsbury and Birkenhead expresses. Through passenger services and through coaches from Birkenhead to the south coast began in the late nineteenth century and carried on well into the twentieth. The line was also always busy with goods traffic. Shrewsbury quickly became a major goods hub with several busy yards and depots in the town. There was a heavy flow of coal traffic from south Wales to Merseyside which passed close to the many collieries around Wrexham. The origin of the route, of course, was the original NWM scheme to connect the heavy industries of north-east Wales to Chester and the rest of the country and branches served the many mines and steel and iron works in that area, bringing additional traffic onto the main line.

By 1850, there were 16 intermediate stations on the 42-mile route. Others, such as those at Johnston & Hafod and Balderton, were added towards the end of the nineteenth century and in the twentieth century the GWR opened a number of halts along the line. At its peak there were 22 stations and halts between Shrewsbury and Chester. Fitting local trains into the working timetables alongside all the goods traffic and the through expresses from London must have been a great challenge to their compilers.

An extant timetable from 1850, shortly after the line opened, shows a total of six trains daily from Shrewsbury to Chester on weekdays. Only two called at all the stations but most omitted only a few calls. Only the first and last trains of the day conveyed third-class passengers. The Regulation of Railways Act of 1844 had forced the reluctant railway companies to run at least one such train a day to provide some facility for the least well off, the so-called Parliamentary trains. The time taken ranged from a lengthy 3 hours and 20 minutes for the first train of the day to a more respectable 1 hour 45 minutes for the quickest. Only two trains ran on the Sabbath, both calling at all stations and conveying all three classes of passengers.

From May 1857 some of the through GWR services from Birmingham to Chester were extended to Birkenhead over the tracks of the Birkenhead Railway. This company was shortly afterwards leased jointly by the GWR and the LNWR and this paved the way to making the Shrewsbury to Chester line part of a through route from the Mersey to the Midlands and London. As mentioned, the commencement of through trains from Birkenhead to Paddington in 1861 increased the importance of the route and added to its traffic. Another flow was introduced to the line in the 1860s with the opening of the railway from Ruabon to Llangollen for goods traffic in December 1861 and passengers in June 1862. By 1868 this line had been extended to Barmouth Junction on the shores of Cardigan Bay. (See *Lost Lines of Wales – Ruabon to Barmouth*, in this series). Most services began and terminated at Ruabon, but latterly some were extended to Chester and even Birkenhead, especially in the summer, as the popularity of the resorts and beaches on the northern shores of Cardigan Bay increased.

The pattern of services established in the mid-nineteenth century century carried on into the twentieth century. A summer timetable from the early 1920s offers six or seven local services in both directions though most of these trains did not cover the whole length of the line, some terminating at Wrexham or Ruabon. There were also through trains and expresses, some conveying dining cars, running from Birkenhead to Birmingham, Leamington Spa or Paddington. In addition, through trains or through carriages to destinations on the south coast were also operated. Up until 1910, all trains to Paddington from Birkenhead and Shrewsbury had had to go via Oxford, a journey sardonically referred to as the Great Way Round. In that year the new Bicester cut off line, which diverged from the Birmingham to Oxford route south of Banbury, opened. This reduced the distance to London by 20 miles and brought Shrewsbury to within under three hours of the capital for the first time, less than 30 minutes slower than the best time offered 100 years later.

The Shrewsbury to Chester line had always carried a healthy freight traffic with trains serving the goods yards of the many stations along the route as well as through goods and mineral trains to Chester and beyond. It should be remembered that the origin of the route was in the NWM scheme to connect the industries and coalfields of north-east Wales and in time branches off the main line, sidings and yards were built to accommodate this, serving places such as Brymbo, Minera and Ffrwd. Another branch diverged at Saltney to wharves on the River Dee. One late addition was the opening in 1921 of a line linking Ifton Colliery to the main line at Weston Rhyn, which at that time was still known by its original name of Preesgweene. At its peak, Ifton Colliery, which closed in 1968, was the largest in Shropshire and employed over 1,000 men.

When British Railways was formed in 1948, the Shrewsbury to Chester line became part of the Western Region, though it was transferred to the London Midland Region in 1963. Many intermediate stations and halts were closed in 1960. All the surviving stations on the line, with the exception of Gobowen, are actually located in Wales. This had the effect of speeding up services and in the mid-1960s the mile per minute timings of some steam hauled trains between Shrewsbury and Gobowen, with the intermediate stations between them having been closed, were among the fastest remaining steam-hauled services in the whole country. The line also had an Indian summer when the West Coast Main Line out of Euston was being electrified in the 1960s. Services on the old GWR route to Birmingham and beyond were increased and accelerated for

a few years, but this all came to an end in March 1967, which saw the end of the through services to Birkenhead.

After that, though still with a reasonable service of trains running from Shrewsbury to Chester and some freight traffic, the line settled down to a pattern of activity still apparent today. The line had been double track throughout its existence until a very short-sighted cost saving exercise undertaken in the 1980s led to the singling of the route between Wrexham and Saltney Junction. This has recently at least been partly mitigated with the completion of work by Network Rail in 2017 to redouble the track on the five-and-a-half-mile stretch between the Rossett and Saltney Junction. Today, some services originating in south Wales run via Shrewsbury beyond Chester to Holyhead and other destinations on the North Wales Coast Line, providing an important link between the north and south of the Principality.

SHREWSBURY

This view of the attractive frontage of Shrewsbury station was taken in August 1962. Designed by Oswestry architect, Thomas Penson, who was also responsible for the other stations on the S&C line, it opened in 1848 and was jointly owned and operated up to the grouping of Britain's railways in 1923 by the GWR and the LNWR, when the latter became part of the London, Midland & Scottish Railway. Remarkably, the bottom level of the building was added about 50 years after the upper two stories had been constructed. At the turn of the twentieth century, in order to expand the facilities, the ground in front of the building was excavated and a new floor was created from the existing cellars and foundations in exactly the same style as that of the existing building.

Trains bound for the Chester line could use either of the two lengthy platforms in this picture, the present-day Platform 3 on which the photographer is standing or Platform 4, where the now preserved No 7827 *Lydham Manor* heads a train of BR MK1 stock. Though these light 4-6-0s were 100% GWR in pedigree, the last ten members of the class, including No 7827, were constructed at the former GWR works at Swindon by BR in 1950. The station was built on a cramped site between Shrewsbury castle, just out of sight behind the trees to the left of the picture, and the River Severn. The southern end of the station rests on three viaducts over the Severn, the original 1840s stone viaduct flanked by later iron and steel constructions added over the years as traffic increased.

Moving to the north end of the station, we see former GWR Hall class 4-6-0 No 6970 *Whaddon Hall* with a service for Chester. The surviving section of the station's overall roof can be seen above the carriages. The northern part of this had been demolished in the 1920s and the remaining southern section was removed in the early 1960s. Today, Shrewsbury is one of the few major centres left on the network where traffic is regulated mostly with traditional semaphore signalling. There is still a signal gantry spanning the tracks, though it now only carries three signals. Whilst track and signalling have been rationalised to some degree, the station is handling more passenger trains now than at any time in its long history. Services from six different routes converge on Shrewsbury, controlled by four signal boxes in the vicinity of the station.

In this 1950s view of the north end of the station, Black Five class 4-6-0 No 44778 pilots an unidentified rebuilt Royal Scot class 4-6-0 on a service for the line to Crewe, which diverges here. Access to this line and that to Chester is still controlled by Crewe Junction signal box, located just beyond the end of Platform 3 on the right of the picture, where an unidentified Black 5 waits for the road. The overall roof referred to earlier can be seen midway down the platform. Another unusual feature is the gantry and pipe just ahead of the loco in Platform 3, which enabled steam engines to top up their water tanks as they waited at the platform.

This photograph taken in 1963 illustrates a change which had occurred at the north end of Shrewsbury station shortly beforehand, the construction of a bridge housing a conveyer belt to allow mail to be easily transferred from the station to the Royal Mail sorting office in Howard Street, to the left of the picture. The exhaust of countless steam locomotives passing under it has already had an effect on its appearance. As well as being a major junction for passenger services, Shrewsbury was an important hub for mail, being served by Travelling Post Office trains for many years. Departing with a passenger train for Chester is ex-GWR Grange class 4-6-0 No 6810 *Blakemere Grange*.

LEATON

Leaton, the first station, was about four miles north of Shrewsbury and was opened with the line by the S&C in 1848. Along with many other stations and halts on the route it was closed to passenger trains in September 1960, though goods services continued until 1965. The signal box, which can be glimpsed by the side of the level crossing gates at the end of the platform, was closed and the level crossing replaced with automatic half barriers in 1987.

OLDWOODS HALT

Just north of Leaton was the first of a number of halts along the route opened by the GWR. Trains began to call at Oldwoods Halt in July 1933. These halts were pretty basic affairs with short timber platforms, wooden shelters for prospective passengers, name boards and oil lamps. As seen here, the halts were usually located beside overbridges which provided passengers with access to the platforms. Oldwoods Halt was closed in September 1960.

BASCHURCH

A local service from Shrewsbury to Chester arrives at Baschurch, hauled by ex-GWR County class 4-6-0 No 1022 *County of Northampton*. Though the station was some distance from the village it served, there have been calls for it to be reopened and there are certainly a lot more people living in Baschurch now than when, with all the other stations and halts between Shrewsbury and Gobowen, it closed in September 1960. Baschurch was the scene of a serious accident in February 1961 when a passenger train bound for Chester struck a goods train being reversed into a siding, resulting in the deaths of three railway workers.

STANWARDINE AND HAUGHTON HALTS

In the four-mile section between Baschurch and the next main station, Rednal, two more halts were provided in the 1930s by the GWR. Stanwardine Halt opened in February 1933 and Haughton in September of the following year. Of similar construction, Haughton's platforms were staggered on either side of the overbridge and it had a siding which remained in situ long after the halt closed in September 1960.

REDNAL AND WEST FELTON

Rednal station opened with the line in October 1848 and succumbed in September 1960. The name of a nearby village, West Felton, was added early in the twentieth century, though the station was not close to either of them. This view, looking north, shows the attractive mock Tudor-style station building, which is still extant, on the Down platform, with the goods yard beyond the signal box.

WHITTINGTON LOW LEVEL

Whittington Low Level opened in 1848 as plain Whittington. Then in July 1864 the village acquired a second station when the Cambrian Railways opened its line from Oswestry to Whitchurch. There were now two Whittington stations on different lines operated by different companies, which must have led to a lot of confusion over the next six decades. It was only after the grouping of Britain's railways in 1923 when the CR was absorbed by the GWR that the former Cambrian station was renamed Whittington High Level and that on the Shrewsbury to Chester line became Whittington Low Level. A train bound for Chester is just passing under the bridge which carried the former CR line as 94XX class Pannier Tank No 3400 arrives at the low level station with a local service heading to Shrewsbury.

GOBOWEN

Gobowen, 18 miles from Shrewsbury, was the junction for the only branch line off the S&C when it opened, just over two miles in length, to Oswestry. The branch is to the right of the train and veers off in the middle distance. Approaching Gobowen on 28th September 1959 is ex-GWR County class 4-6-0 No 1013 *County of Dorset*. Introduced in 1945 to the design of the company's last Chief Mechanical Engineer, F. W. Hawksworth, this was the last new type of 4-6-0 built by the GWR, the final evolution of a family of locomotives which dated back to the early 1900s.

Pausing at Gobowen on 28th September 1959 with the 4.30pm through train from Birkenhead to Paddington is ex-GWR Hall class 4-6-0 No 5930 *Hannington Hall*, one of the 330 members of this successful class of mixed traffic locomotives, the first of which entered service in 1924.

On 30th May 1961, ex-GWR Pannier Tank No 6419 propels the 2.55pm two-coach Autotrain to Oswestry out of Gobowen. The GWR used this method of operation extensively on branch lines across its system. When the loco was leading, both driver and fireman were on the footplate as normal, but when the carriages were being propelled, as here, the driver was in a cab at the end of the leading carriage. He could regulate the train's speed via mechanical rodding running under the coaches linked to controls on the loco and apply the brakes. The fireman remained on the loco, dealing with the fire and water. This meant that the engine did not have to uncouple and run round the train at termini, which saved a lot of time.

OSWESTRY

At the other end of the branch, in its bay platform at Oswestry on 23rd February 1962, auto-fitted ex-GWR 0-4-2 Tank No 1432 waits to haul its two-coach Autotrain back to Gobowen. The branch closed in November 1966, the final passenger service to Oswestry, which had been a major railway centre, headquarters of the Cambrian Railways and home of their locomotive works. The former CR line from Welshpool to Whitchurch had closed the previous year. The branch from Gobowen was used by BR into the late 1980s to convey ballast from a quarry at Blodwell beyond Oswestry and is still in existence. Cambrian Heritage Railways, a preservation scheme, is based at Oswestry now and the hope remains that some day the branch will be revived, though its level crossing over the busy A5 road could well be the major impediment to that.

WESTON RHYN

Despite the increasing prevalence of Welsh-sounding names around Gobowen and Oswestry, the Shrewsbury to Chester line is still running through England until just south of Chirk. The first station north of Gobowen was Weston Rhyn. When it opened in 1848 it was known as Presgwyn, later changed to Preesgwyn and finally Preesgwyn for Weston Rhyn, though some timetables spelt this as Preesgweene, highlighting, if it needs highlighting, what a minefield the spelling of anglicised Welsh place names is. Eventually, it became plain Weston Rhyn in the 1930s. At the station, the main line was joined by a branch serving the first colliery on the line thus far. The line to Ifton colliery trailed in behind the approaching southbound passenger train in the picture. The colliery, which opened in the 1920s, employed at its peak 1,300 men and was the most productive coal mine in Shropshire, closing in November 1968.

CHIRK VIADUCT

There was barely a mile between Weston Rhyn and the next station, Chirk, but in that short distance the line both passed from England into Wales and crossed one of its most impressive feats of engineering. Both the railway and the Llangollen canal before it had to pass over the valley of the River Ceiriog. Thomas Telford's canal aqueduct was completed in 1801 and Henry Robertson's viaduct for the S&C in 1848. It was 100ft high with ten stone spans and stands some 30ft above the adjacent canal aqueduct. It is almost a metaphor in stone for how the railways eclipsed and ultimately replaced the canals as the major transport arteries of the country. Normally in this series, we try to steer away from pictures of special trains to focus on the day-to-day activity on the lines being covered, however, this view not only shows off the viaduct

and aqueduct at Chirk to good effect, it brings back particular memories for me in that I was very fortunate to have been invited to be a passenger on this very special 'special', which ran on 18th October 1986 and was organised to mark the 80th birthday of one of the great railway photographers of the last century, W. A. Camwell, whose images have graced this series. The four-coach special train was hauled by the sole surviving, out of 300 built between 1881 and 1897, London & North Western Railway 0-6-2 'Coal Tank' LNWR No 1054, which at that time was permitted to travel on the main lines.

Passengers arriving at Chirk between 1888 and 1935 could not have failed to notice the town's other railway, which terminated adjacent to the main line station. This was the Glyn Valley Tramway, a 2ft 4½in narrow-gauge line that ran 8 miles up the Ceiriog valley to serve granite and slate quarries there. From 1891 until 1933 passenger services were operated from Chirk over 6½ miles of the line as far as Glyn Ceiriog. Declining goods traffic and mounting losses led to the line finally closing in 1935.

Opposite page: The Tramway's engine shed was at Chirk and the three original 0-4-2T locomotives built by Beyer Peacock are shown there sometime after 1892, when the first two locos were joined by a third, *Glyn*, the one in the centre of the trio. On the left is *Dennis* and behind *Sir Theodore*, both dating from 1888. Because the tramway ran alongside the public road for much of the way, the locos' motions were encased in skirts to protect other road users.

Above left: In 1921, an additional loco was acquired. This was an American Baldwin 4-6-0T built in 1917 for use by the War Department on the vast network of narrow-gauge railways used to supply the trenches in northern France during the First World War.

Left: The Baldwin is seen again in this view of some stone wagons at the narrow-gauge platform at Chirk, which was adjacent to that for main line trains bound for Chester.

CHIRK STATION

Northbound trains entered Chirk station 21 miles from Shrewsbury shortly after leaving the short tunnel at the end of the viaduct. The attractive main buildings on the Up platform were demolished in the 1980s, replaced by a modest shelter for passengers.

A siding on the Up side of the line just north of the station served a Cadbury factory for many years. It is now used to access the Kronospan wood products plant. Freight trains bringing timber to the factory from various parts of the country still run on a regular basis.

WHITEHURST HALT

When the line opened in 1848, a station called Llangollen Road was provided a mile or so north of Chirk, close to the Holyhead road, to act as a railhead for Llangollen about five miles distant. This closed when the line from Ruabon to Llangollen opened in 1862, but close to the site of the former station Whitehurst Halt was opened in 1905. It differed from the 1930s-built halts further south in that it had longer platforms and instead of wooden shelters, it was provided with distinctive corrugated iron 'pagoda'-style shelters for passengers. These were a feature of many halts built by the GWR across its network.

A mile beyond Whitehurst Halt the tracks passed over the second great engineering achievement of the Shrewsbury to Chester line, Cefn viaduct. Like Thomas Telford's nearby masterpiece, the Pontcysyllte aqueduct on the Llangollen canal, the viaduct was required to span the valley of the River Dee. Designed by Henry Robertson and built by Thomas Brassey, it took two years to complete. The structure has 19 arches, is 1,508ft in length and rises 150ft above the river.

CEFN STATION

Whilst Cefn viaduct was under construction, the line south from Wrexham terminated at a temporary station at Rhosymedre. This was replaced in 1849 with a permanent one at Cefn, which remained open until the mass station closures of 1960. A southbound stopping passenger train arrives at Cefn, headed by a rather grubby ex-GWR Hall class locomotive, No 6928 *Underley Hall*.

LLANGOLLEN JUNCTION

Just south of Ruabon was Llangollen Junction, where this lengthy and picturesque line though Mid Wales to the shores of Cardigan Bay built in the 1860s diverged from the Shrewsbury to Chester route. (See the book in this series, *Lost Lines of Wales – Ruabon to Barmouth*.) Former LMS Black Five class 4-6-0 No 45184 on a service from Shrewsbury to Chester passes the junction. The line had double track as far as Llangollen and single beyond there and closed in January 1965.

RUABON

Ruabon was a large station with three platforms, the one to the left on which the photographer was positioned being an island platform. Here ex-GWR Hall class No 6937 *Conyngham Hall* arrives from the Wrexham direction with a passenger train.

On 30th May 1961, a service for Barmouth headed by ex-GWR 2-6-0 No 7314 is ready to depart. Trains to Llangollen and beyond usually used this platform at Ruabon, though some of the workings off this line ran through to Chester or Birkenhead, especially in summer, to cater for holiday traffic to the many resorts on the shores of Cardigan Bay.

WYNNVILLE HALT

North of Ruabon, the railway entered that heavily industrialised part of north-east Wales whose transport needs had encouraged its original promotion back in the 1840s. Numerous branches and sidings to collieries and factories were a feature of the next part of the route. To serve a settlement on the northern outskirts of Ruabon, Wynnville Halt was opened in February 1934 and lasted until September 1960. As with the other halts opened in the 1930s along the line, it was a very modest structure with wooden shelters and platforms accessed by steps on either side of the road bridge.

JOHNSTOWN AND HAFOD

Johnstown & Hafod, less than two miles north of Ruabon, was opened as a station in 1896, conveniently close to an adjacent colliery. It was downgraded to the status of a halt in 1955 and its nameboard was altered accordingly. Like so many other stopping places on the line, it finally succumbed to the great cull of September 1960. In this undated 1950s view, ex-GWR 0-6-0 Pannier Tank No 4617, one of 852 of these locos, by far the most numerous GWR class ever built, arrives with a southbound stopping passenger train.

CROES NEWYDD SHED

Situated on the southern approaches to Wrexham was the triangular junction at Croes Newydd, with a signal box at each apex. The Shrewsbury to Chester line formed one part of the triangle, north and south-facing connections from the lines to Brymbo the others. In the centre of this triangle was the large Croes Newydd engine shed. Opened by the GWR in 1902, it consisted of a roundhouse, with a central turntable inside with sidings off this for the locomotives. Croes Newydd had an allocation of 54 locos in 1950 and it also had smaller sub sheds under its wing at Bala, Trawsfyndd and Penmaenpool. Coded CNYD by the GWR, its BR shed code

from 1949 to 1960 was 84J, changing to 89B from 1960 to 1963 when it passed from the Western Region to the London Midland and was reclassified by them to 6C. It was the last BR shed to have ex-GWR locos on its books and finally closed in 1967. In this undated 1950s view, ex-GWR locomotives predominate with three types of Pannier Tank represented, along with a 28XX class 2-8-0 and a 2251 class 0-6-0. One ex-

LMS type, an 8F 2-8-0, is behind No 7409, to the right of the ramp leading to the shed's coaling stage, which is topped by another essential of any big shed, a large water tank.

Above left: A later view, looking inside the roundhouse, shows BR Standard class 4-6-0 No 75021 being turned by muscle power on the shed's turntable.

Above right: Some of the residents of the shed recorded in August 1964 are grouped around the turntable; those identifiable from left to right include ex-GWR 2-8-0 No 3813, BR Standard class 4 4-6-0 No 75023 and BR Standard class 4 2-6-4T No 80080, the latter being one of the fortunate ones which were subsequently preserved.

The rear of the main building of Croes Newydd shed is on the left of this picture which looks along the Shrewsbury to Chester line towards Croes Newydd North Junction. The southbound goods train running under clear signals is hauled by an early member of the ex-GWR Hall class, No 4918 *Dartington Hall.*

This 1965 view taken from the trackside shows a northbound passenger train headed by ex-LMS Black 5 4-6-0 No 45353 passing Croes Newydd North Fork signal box.

WREXHAM GENERAL

Dating from 1846, as befitting an important railway and industrial centre, Wrexham's main station, Wrexham General, was substantially rebuilt by the GWR in 1910-12. It had long through platforms and bay platforms at its south end. Beside the GWR station was Wrexham Exchange – this was opened in 1866 by the Wrexham, Mold & Connah's Quay Railway, later taken over by the Great Central Railway and in turn, at the 1923 grouping of Britain's railways, it became an outpost of the London & North Eastern Railway. Trains still run from Wrexham's third station, Wrexham Central, through the remaining platform at what was Wrexham Exchange, to Bidston on the Wirral. A Birkenhead to Paddington train headed by ex-GWR Hall class 4-6-0 No 4944 *Middleton Hall* arrives at the lengthy Up platform at Wrexham General. The footbridge provided a link to Wrexham Exchange, the former LNER station.

A southbound goods train runs through Wrexham General hauled by ex-LMS Black 5 4-6-0 No 45198 passing the large buildings to the right which were part of Wrexham General's goods depot.

This view of the south end of the GWR station in Wrexham probably dates from the 1920s. An unidentified Saint class 4-6-0 heads a Chester to Shrewsbury train, but of equal interest is the stock in the bay platform; this consists of one of the GWR's Steam Rail Motors. These were carriages self propelled by a small internal steam engine – its stub chimney can just be seen protruding at the front of the vehicle. Capable of hauling a trailer, they were first introduced in 1903 to cut costs and provide more frequent services on both rural branch lines and those in urban centres where electric street tramways were making inroads into the railway's passenger numbers. There were still many in service in the 1920s, though they had all been withdrawn by 1935. Some of the carriages were converted to run as auto-trailers (see pages 27 and 28) and a number of these remained in service well into the British Railways era.

Heading north out of Wrexham, a halt was opened in 1932 at Rhosrobin to serve both the settlement of that name and nearby Gresford Colliery, though it only lasted until 1947. Gresford Colliery, which closed in 1973, was the scene of one of Britain's worst mining disasters, an underground explosion on Saturday 22nd September 1935 which led to the deaths of 266 men. The colliery with its winding gear is in the background in this view of a Birkenhead to Paddington express headed by ex-LMS class 5 4-6-0 No 44912.

GRESFORD

Gresford station, three miles north of Wrexham, dated from the opening of this part of the line in 1846. Its main buildings were situated on the Up platform, though for those with an interest in railways its name is usually associated with the notorious Gresford bank, over three miles long on a gradient of 1 in 82, of which the station marked roughly the midpoint. Declining passenger numbers led to it being downgraded to the status of a halt in 1955 when its name was also changed to that shown here, Gresford for Llay Halt. It briefly survived the station closures of 1960, finally losing its remaining sparse service in September 1962.

A stiff incline, such as Gresford bank, presented several operational challenges in the age of steam. The obvious one was that of locomotives losing grip and stalling as they slogged uphill, but there was also the danger of wagon couplings breaking. The vast majority of steam age goods wagons did not have continuous brakes operated from the locomotive, they were provided with only handbrakes so if the couplings snapped part of the train could career downhill with only the hand brake in the Guard's van to slow them. At Gresford station, any such runaways could be diverted by the signalman into the siding on the left of the picture to avert a collision with a following train. This view of a goods train hauled by ex-GWR 2-8-0 No 2878 gingerly descending the bank on 9th May 1949 illustrates another potential hazard. As the only brake power for the train was supplied by the locomotive and the Guard's van at the end, goods trains often had to stop at the top of an incline to allow the Guard to pin down the handbrakes on some of the wagons to prevent the train running out of control as it headed downhill.

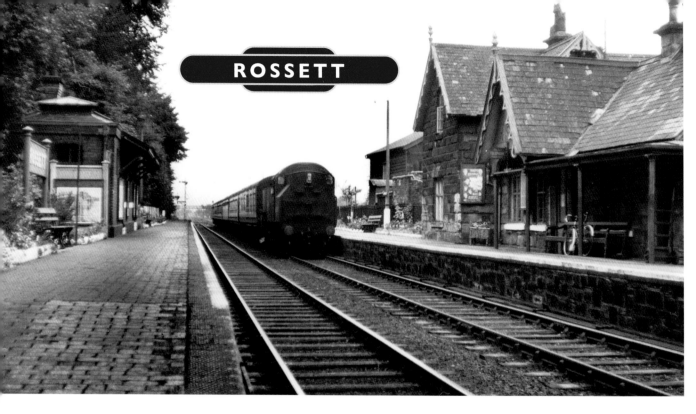

ROSSETT

Rossett station opened with the first part of the line in 1846 and was finally closed in October 1964. The main buildings were on the Up platform where a local service hauled by an unidentified former LMS 2-6-4T is preparing to stop. Rossett was on the part of the line which was reduced to a single track in 1983 though the double track was restored by Network Rail, the work being completed in April 2017.

BALDERTON

Between Rossett and the next station about three miles to the north of it, Balderton, the railway crossed back into England. There had been another station on this stretch of the line, just inside Cheshire at Pulford which opened in 1846, but just to prove that station closures were not just a twentieth-century phenomenon, it was closed in 1855. Balderton opened in 1901 but lost its passenger trains in 1952. This view, dating from before April 1933 when the loco was withdrawn, shows Churchward designed GWR County class 4-4-0 No 3822 *County of Brecon* passing through the station on a milk train.

SALTNEY

The final station on the line before its junction with the route from Chester to Holyhead was at Saltney, which in its heyday was an important place.

The station itself had a chequered history, opening in November 1846 and closing in January 1917 as a wartime economy measure though much of its passenger traffic had been already lost to Chester's trams since the route terminating close to the station was electrified in 1904. The second

Saltney station, pictured here, though with its staggered wooden platforms it had more of the appearance of a halt, was opened by the GWR in July 1932 and retained a passenger service until 1960. This view from the BR era shows a southbound passenger service hauled by ex-GWR 2-6-0 No 6357 at the Up platform.

SALTNEY DEE JUNCTION

Just to the south of the station, a branch dating from the opening of the line in 1846 diverged to serve wharves on the River Dee. Saltney Dee Junction signal box controlled the junction and this delightful late nineteenth-century view shows some of the staff posing for the camera in the company of a GWR 0-4-0 Saddle Tank. In the space between the main line and the branch the S&C established a locomotive works in 1847 and under the GWR this was transformed into a facility to build carriages and goods wagons housed in the lengthy buildings behind the signal box. This short branch down to the Dee originally carried large volumes of coal, iron and other traffic, but with the silting of the river and the decline of Chester as a port this fell away, the branch finally being abandoned by BR in 1970.

Saltney Junction was where the line from Shrewsbury joined that from Chester to Holyhead (see *Lost Lines of Wales – Chester to Holyhead* in this series). S&C trains were actually the first to use this part of the North Wales Coast route, when their services commenced in November 1846. It would be May 1848 before the first 60 miles of the Chester & Holyhead Railway opened for traffic. Between 1903 and 1979 there were four tracks over the just under two-mile section from Saltney Junction to Chester General station. Here a service for Shrewsbury headed by ex-GWR Hall class 4-6-0 No 6938 *Corndean Hall* passes the LNWR style signal box which controlled the junction.

There was one final engineering feature on the route before it reached the confines of Chester General station – this was the bridge which carried the railway lines over the River Dee. On a murky morning in April 1957, ex-GWR Castle class 4-6-0 No 5050

Earl of St Germans heads a Birkenhead to Paddington train across the bridge. The collapse of the original bridge on 24th May 1847, taking a S&C train to Ruabon with it and leading to the deaths of five people, came close to ending the illustrious career of

Robert Stephenson, the C&H engineer. The subsequent Board of Trade enquiry into the collapse placed the blame squarely on his design for the structure.

CHESTER

A short passenger train bound for the Shrewsbury line leaves Chester, passing Chester No 6 signal box perched on a gantry over the tracks.

The signalling and the many signal boxes at Chester were of LNWR origin. The lines to the left of the picture allowed trains heading to and from

Birkenhead off the lines approaching Chester from the west to bypass the station and avoid reversal there.

A parcels and van train off the Birkenhead line hauled by ex-GWR Hall class loco No 6924 *Grantley Hall* arrives at Chester and passes another of the large LNWR designed signal boxes, which handled traffic movements at Chester station and its environs. Chester No 4 controlled the junction of the lines to Holyhead and Shrewsbury with those to Birkenhead.

In its heyday in the steam era, before the railway network began to contract and much loved steam engines were replaced by diesel and electric locomotives and multiple units, Chester, like Shrewsbury at the other end of our line, at this time would have been a fascinating place for railway enthusiasts. From Chester, famously, passengers heading for London could board expresses which began their journeys by travelling in the opposite direction to each other. The trains for Paddington via Shrewsbury went west out of Chester General, those bound for Euston going east via Crewe.

As this is a book about a line whose history and pedigree was that of the Great Western and latterly the Western Region of British Railways for over 100 years, it is appropriate to end with a view of a former GWR locomotive.

Manor class 4-6-0 No 7801 *Anthony Manor* was built at Swindon Works in 1938, the second member of its class; the locomotive remained in service until July 1965, when she was withdrawn from Shrewsbury shed. The Manors were the lightest of the GWR family of 4-6-0s and were used extensively on the former Cambrian lines from Ruabon to Barmouth and from Shrewsbury to Aberystwyth and along to Cambrian coast to Pwllheli. The presence of No 7801 at the west end of Chester station suggests she was likely to be rostered for a working to Ruabon and then on to the coast via Llangollen. The locomotive, resplendent in lined green BR livery, cannot have been long out of the works after an overhaul and carries an 89A shed plate on her smokebox denoting that she was based at Oswestry at this time, having moved there from the West Country in March 1959.

CREDITS

Lost Lines of England and Wales – Shrewsbury to Chester. Published in Great Britain in 2021 by Graffeg Limited.

Written by Tom Ferris copyright © 2021. Designed and produced by Graffeg Limited copyright © 2021.

Graffeg Limited, 24 Stradey Park Business Centre, Mwrwg Road, Llangennech, Llanelli, Carmarthenshire, SA14 8YP, Wales, UK. Tel 01554 824000. www.graffeg.com.

Tom Ferris is hereby identified as the author of this work in accordance with section 77 of the Copyrights, Designs and Patents Act 1988.

A CIP Catalogue record for this book is available from the British Library.

ISBN 9781914079122

1 2 3 4 5 6 7 8 9

MIX
Paper from responsible sources
FSC® C014138
www.fsc.org

Photo credits

© John Mc Cann/Online Transport Archive: page 13.
© Great Western Trust: pages 15, 16, 19, 21, 22, 32, 35, 39, 46, 48, 50, 54, 55, 58, 60.
© W. A. C. Smith/Transport Treasury: pages 17, 25, 26.
© Paul Riley/ Kidderminster Railway Museum: pages 18, 47.
© Michael Hale/Great Western Trust: pages 20, 23, 24, 29, 37, 42, 43, 45 (left), 52, 56.
© Transport Treasury: pages 27, 28, 41, 44, 49, 61, 63.
© SLS Collection: page 30.
© Tom Ferris: pages 33, 34, 36.
© M Roberts/Kidderminster Railway Museum: page 40.
© Ian Krause/Kidderminster Railway Museum: pages 45, 51.
© P M Alexander/ Kidderminster Railway Museum: page 53.
© Online Transport Archive: pages 57, 59.

The photographs used in this book have come from a variety of sources. Wherever possible contributors have been identified although some images may have been used without credit or acknowledgement and if this is the case apologies are offered and full credit will be given in any future edition.

Cover: Chirk Viaduct.
Back cover: The Glyn Valley Tramway, Oswestry, Chester.

Lost Lines of England:

The Cheddar Valley Line ISBN 9781913134402
Birmingham to Oxford ISBN 9781912654871
Ryde to Cowes ISBN 9781912654864

Lost Lines of England and Wales:

Shrewsbury to Chester ISBN 9781914079122

Lost Lines of Wales series:

Cambrian Coast Line ISBN 9781909823204
Aberystwyth to Carmarthen ISBN 9781909823198
Brecon to Newport ISBN 9781909823181
Ruabon to Barmouth ISBN 9781909823174
Chester to Holyhead ISBN 9781912050697
Shrewsbury to Aberystwyth ISBN 9781912050680
The Mid Wales Line ISBN 9781912050673
Vale of Neath ISBN 9781912050666
Rhyl to Corwen ISBN 9781912213108
Bangor to Afon Wen ISBN 9781912213115
The Heads of the Valleys Line ISBN 9781912654154
Conwy Valley Line ISBN 9781912654147
Llandovery to Craven Arms ISBN 9781914079115
Swansea to Llandovery ISBN 9781914079108